THIS IS ME!

ACROSTICS

Poetry Gems

Edited By Roseanna Caswell

First published in Great Britain in 2022 by:

 YoungWriters® Est. 1991

Young Writers
Remus House
Coltsfoot Drive
Peterborough
PE2 9BF
Telephone: 01733 890066
Website: www.youngwriters.co.uk

Printed and bound in the UK by BookPrintingUK
Website: www.bookprintinguk.com
YB0506R

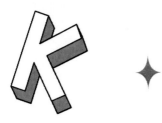

Foreword

Welcome Reader,

For Young Writers' latest competition *This Is Me Acrostics*, we asked primary school pupils to look inside themselves, to think about what makes them unique, and then write an acrostic poem about it! They rose to the challenge magnificently and the result is this fantastic collection of poems, celebrating them and the things that are important to them.

Here at Young Writers our aim is to encourage creativity in children and to inspire a love of the written word, so it's great to get such an amazing response, with some absolutely fantastic poems. It's important for children to focus on and celebrate themselves and this competition allowed them to write freely and honestly, celebrating what makes them great, expressing their hopes and fears, or simply writing about their favourite things. *This Is Me Acrostics* gave them the power of words.

I'd like to congratulate all the young poets in this anthology, I hope this inspires them to continue with their creative writing.

Contents

Our Lady Of Lourdes Catholic Primary School, Finchley

Sofia Vento (7)	57
Gabriele Marroccu (7)	58
Patrick McErlean (7)	59
Nicolas Junev (6)	60
Albert May (7)	61
Nina Nyangeri (6)	62

Overstone Park School, Northampton

Lilly Doyle (7)	63
Dera Okafor (7)	64
Spencer Nathwani (7)	65
Mitchell Maskell (7)	66
Jasmine Filbee (7)	67
Hannah Mabuto (7)	68
Beaux Downing (7)	69
Shamar Hall (5)	70
Garry Denton (5)	71

Prestwich Preparatory School, Prestwich

Abdur-Raheem Khan (6)	72
Hashim Zia (6)	73
Taaliah Hamid (5)	74
Isla Gorman (6)	75
Nkosi Kubekwani (6)	76
Zayan Hussain (7)	77
Samuel Dirawu (7)	78
Zaya Owoyomi (5)	79

St Blasius CE Primary Academy, Shanklin

Amber Milewska (7)	80
Nela Biesaga (6)	81
Isla Lind (7)	82
Santiago Montenegro (6)	83
Beatrice Thomas (6)	84
Lincoln Newton (7)	85
Jed Smith (6)	86

Malachi Carman (7)	87
Rosie Kenny (6)	88
William Nicol (6)	89
Rhys Antoine-Neilson (6)	90
Elijah Simpson-Little (7)	91
Lacie-Mae Firth (7)	92
Thomas Davey (6)	93
Olivia Borkiewicz (7)	94
Fred Fry (6)	95
Lola Chambers (6)	96
Hugo Crates (7)	97
Ely Orchard (7)	98

Thomas Whitehead CE Academy, Houghton Regis

Emily Keeler (7)	99
Eva Deme Dluhosova (7)	100
Olivia-Mae Bogart (6)	101
Cameron Vickers (6)	102
Samuel Dagnall (6)	103
Kayleigh Shumbambiri (6)	104
Finley Long (6)	105
Kaiya Levey (6)	106
Mia Taylor (6)	107
Lily (6)	108
Scarlett Casey (6)	109
Millie Hedges (5)	110
Bailey Spencer Kennedy (6)	111
Erik Elek (5)	112
Ariana Rose Noka (6)	113
Darian Ukoh (5)	114
Michael Magnan (5)	115
Jayda Hart (7)	116
Kadie Lowe (6)	117

Ysgol Ffordd Dyffryn, Llandudno

William Sowtus (7)	118
Martha Guiney (6)	119
Gabriel Rodrigues (6)	120
Louie Kincaid (7)	121
Barry Palin (6)	122
Olly Owen (7)	123

The
Acrostics

Kyle Baliikya

K yle, me, is the fastest in the class
Y oghurt is my favourite
L ucky four-leaf clovers are my favourite
E njoys football

B alls make me want to kick one
A wesome is my job
L ollies make me hungry
I ncredible things are cool
I nteresting things surprise me
K yle, me, is the coolest boy in class
Y oung people are like me
A mazing things interest me.

Kyle Baliikya (7)
Deanwood Primary School, Parkwood

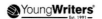

This Is Me, Alf

T he luckiest boy in the world
H elicopters are so cool
I love Miss White and Miss Toombs
S ister is Bella

I love chocolate cake with toffee on
S chool is the best

M e... I really love me
E pic I am

A lfie, which is me
L uke who is my dad
F ortnite!

Alfie Francis (6)
Deanwood Primary School, Parkwood

Emily Poem

W hat am I doing?

A t my mum's I have watermelon

T o

E at

R ats, I have lots at my home

M um helps me

E lf is naughty

L ucky girl

O ften at school

N o, I nearly fell over.

Emily Airey (6)

Deanwood Primary School, Parkwood

I Like Cats

I love Mikey

L ove animals
O ranges are good
V ans are cool
E njoys drawing

M ikey likes trees
I am incredible
K ey opens doors
E njoys cats
Y ears are long.

Alexandra Ivy Offord (7)
Deanwood Primary School, Parkwood

Fornite

F ortnite
O range is my second favourite colour
R ed is cool
T itans are big robots
N ights are awesome
I mpressive
T he wickedest boy in the world
E ating all the time.

Oliver Baker (6)

Deanwood Primary School, Parkwood

I Am A Gamer

I love my Switch

A mazing gamer
M aster

A ctive boy

G amer
A wesome
M aking
E njoy me now
R ap.

Alfie Henderson
Deanwood Primary School, Parkwood

Happy

H appy when it's Christmas

A pples with the skin off

P laying with my toys

P okémon is my favourite

Y oghurt is my favourite.

Loui Wood (5)

Deanwood Primary School, Parkwood

Gamer

G aming is fun, really fun

A nimals are precious

M ummy is funny

E verybody is amazing

R ed is my favourite colour. Red is good.

Lincoln O'Donovan (6)
Deanwood Primary School, Parkwood

Pets

F ishes are pretty

I love you

S he likes to slither

H ollie is my friend

E ggs are tasty

S weets are the best.

Sophie Flatt (5)

Deanwood Primary School, Parkwood

Enderman

E ggs and soldiers

N intendo Switch

D addy

E njoys football

R aps

M ummy

A mazing

N ice.

Oliver Darlington (7)
Deanwood Primary School, Parkwood

Callum's Poem

S chool is the best

C hocolate is my favourite

H ens I love

O ranges are tasty

O ranges are good

L ove owls.

Callum Kennedy (6)

Deanwood Primary School, Parkwood

Kind

K ind is helpful to you
I 'm incredible at home and play games
N ight is like space but even cooler
D oes the right thing.

Edward Stairs (6)
Deanwood Primary School, Parkwood

Blue

B lueberries are my favourite food
L oving is a good thing
U nbelievable with excitement
E xciting times are with us.

Millie Pullen (6)

Deanwood Primary School, Parkwood

Aleeya Poem

S now is my favourite
N aughty snow is messy
O ften, I will get to play
W hite snow comes down from the sky.

Aleeya-Mae Carpenter (5)
Deanwood Primary School, Parkwood

Happy

H i, my name is Harley

A friend is good

P eople are funny

P eople are good

Y ou are kind.

Harley Sharpe (6)

Deanwood Primary School, Parkwood

Matilda Poem

C ats I have
A nd one is called Lily
T he other one is Avery
S o, I like playing with her.

Matilda Holmes (5)
Deanwood Primary School, Parkwood

Book

B londe hair
O range is my favourite
O ak Class, I love you
K ind is what I like to be.

Evelyn Ball (6)

Deanwood Primary School, Parkwood

Callum Poem

C ool
A ctive
L ol
L uca is my best friend
U nstoppable
M ummy.

Callum Watts (6)
Deanwood Primary School, Parkwood

Ella's Poem

S now is cold

N ew snow is fun

O nce, I played in the snow

W here I made a snowman.

Ella Cairns (6)

Deanwood Primary School, Parkwood

Snow

S now is soft
"N o!" said Mum
O h no! My toy broke
W here are we?

Joshua Batther (5)
Deanwood Primary School, Parkwood

Pet

R uby is my dog

U sually good

B lack fur

Y ou are very good.

Harry Hewish-Osborne (5)

Deanwood Primary School, Parkwood

Lily

L ovely city

I love my family

L ove Selena

Y ay! Home time!

Lily Hastings-Thorpe (7)
Deanwood Primary School, Parkwood

Cool

C reative
O range is my favourite colour
O nly seven
L olly.

Lenny-Shai Stevenson-Delaney (7)

Deanwood Primary School, Parkwood

Snow

S now is cold
N ew Year is fun
O n your bottom
W atch TV.

Betsy Stevenson (5)
Deanwood Primary School, Parkwood

Seaside

S easide is beautiful
U mbrella for the rain
N ice place to be
L ying on the beach
I like to play in the sand
G irls and boys playing
H ot days on the beach
T he sun makes me happy.

Blen Berhe (6)
Fairchildes Primary School, New Addington

Flower

F lower is lonely
L ittle flowers on the grass
O range and blue flowers are my favourite
W et flowers in the rain
E veryone loves flowers
R ain makes the flowers grow.

Mohamed Mohamed (6)

Fairchildes Primary School, New Addington

Football

F ootball is my hobby

O ffside

O ne day I will be a famous player

T he ball is bouncing

B all

A football match

L ose

L ove football.

Alex Kocia (6)

Fairchildes Primary School, New Addington

Animal

A nts are tiny

N ests are for birds

I nsects are small

M ice have lots of babies

A pes are monkeys

L ions roar very loudly.

Jorgie Brown (6)
Fairchildes Primary School, New Addington

Friend

F unny faces

R unning with my friend

I love my friend

E njoying playing

N ice friends are good

D ad is my friend.

Leo Wicking (5)

Fairchildes Primary School, New Addington

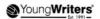

Teagan

T eagan
E njoys
A rt and
G oing to the beach with family
A long with her family
N othing is boring.

Teagan Hewitt (8)

Fairchildes Primary School, New Addington

Mummy

M ummy is the best
U nder the rainbow
M y favourite person ever
M akes me a cup of tea
Y um, yum!

Tanniya Quarry-Flynn (6)
Fairchildes Primary School, New Addington

Kian

K icking my football
I am going to the park
A t home, I play
N ext morning I have a match.

Kian Spillane-Erb (6)

Fairchildes Primary School, New Addington

The Beach

S harks can be found
W aves at the beach
I get wet
M um helps me swim.

Marios Jones (5)
Fairchildes Primary School, New Addington

Family

M y family
I love my family
A nd they are kind.

Mia Shirley (5)
Fairchildes Primary School, New Addington

Fall

F resh
A pple
L ots
L eaves.

Arooj Sohail Chaudhary (6)

Fairchildes Primary School, New Addington

Trustworthy

T ry to be trustworthy

R eally try hard

U se your kindest heart

S ee who can trust you

T ell the truth

W ill you keep my secrets

O r not?

R eally be a good friend

T hat I can trust

H eroes are trustworthy

Y ou can be trustworthy like me.

Barbara Ingram (6)
Oakwood Primary School, Easter House

Beautiful

B eautiful is not just how you look
E veryone can be kind
A nd help other people
U nderstand people are different
T hat is being beautiful inside
I am beautiful inside and out
F orgive other people
U nderstand their mistakes
L et us all be beautiful.

Harlie Milligan (6)
Oakwood Primary School, Easter House

Courageous

C an you be brave like me?

O nly heroes can be brave

U ntrue!

R eally, anyone can be brave

A nd courageous

G o for it!

E veryone can try

O ut the box thinking

U ntil you try, you won't know

S ee if you really are brave.

George McQuade (6)

Oakwood Primary School, Easter House

Marvellous

M y name is Zach
A nd I try to be marvellous
R eally, I try to be amazing
V ery good and kind
E veryone says I'm cool
L ike my uncle David
L ike my dad
O ne of the best
U sually, I am marvellous
S ometimes I am not!

Zach McGinlay (6)
Oakwood Primary School, Easter House

Adorable

A dorable, that is me
D reams of princesses are adorable
O nce I saw an adorable bunny
R ainbows in the sky are adorable
A dorable, that is my sister too
B ut you need to be kind
L oving other people so
E veryone can be adorable like me.

Iris Lin (6)
Oakwood Primary School, Easter House

Athletic

A thletic is being sporty

T ime to get fit

H ow many push-ups can you do?

L eap up like a kangaroo

E very time you can do a sit-up

T ennis is a good game to play

I like to play basketball

C an you be athletic like me?

Rory Smith (6)

Oakwood Primary School, Easter House

Superstar

S hine like a superstar
U se your brain
P ush yourself to do your best
E xcellent add sums
R eally good writing
S uper art
T errific singing
A mazing in all ways
R eady to be a superstar.

Anaya Khan (6)
Oakwood Primary School, Easter House

Creative

C an you be creative like me?
R ainbows full of colour
E ach design is different
A rt is always fun
T ime to be yourself
I love to be creative
V ery, very creative
E very chance I have.

Katerina Spanellis (6)
Oakwood Primary School, Easter House

Artistic

A rt is so much fun
R ainbows of colour
T each me how to draw
I see patterns and shapes
S o many ideas
T o draw and to paint
I love being artistic
C reative ideas fill my head.

Olivia Corbett (6)
Oakwood Primary School, Easter House

Helpful

H ailey is my name and I am helpful
E veryone can be helpful
L et me tell you how
P lease tidy up
F ollow the rules
U nderstand you must lend a hand
L et me help you.

Hailey Sheppard (6)
Oakwood Primary School, Easter House

Playful

P laying is fun
L ife can be cool if you play
A nd are playful
Y ou can laugh
F ind a good game
U se your smile
L et's have fun!

Charli Cox (6)
Oakwood Primary School, Easter House

Honest

H elp people to be honest

O ur school values honesty

N ever tell lies

E veryone must try

S ometimes it's hard

T ymoteusz is honest.

Tymoteusz Widelski (7)

Oakwood Primary School, Easter House

Capable

C ooper is my name
A lways joking
P laying football
A nd helping others
B eing capable
L ove being outside
E njoying life!

Lucas Cooper (6)
Oakwood Primary School, Easter House

Lovely

L ovely is being kind

O ur house is lovely

V ases of flowers are lovely

E veryone can be lovely

L et's try hard

Y ou can do it!

Kayla Brothers (6)

Oakwood Primary School, Easter House

Sporty

S port is the best
P laying football is fantastic
O r basketball
R ugby is so cool
T ennis can be tricky
Y ou know I am sporty.

Jordan Bovill (6)
Oakwood Primary School, Easter House

Funny

F unny things make me laugh
U nderstand I like a joke
N ever stop me from having fun
N ow I like to play a trick
Y es, I am a funny boy!

Josh Allison (6)
Oakwood Primary School, Easter House

Brave

B eing brave can be hard
R eally very hard
A lways try your best and
V ery often you will see
E veryone can be brave like me.

Daniel Roderickson (6)
Oakwood Primary School, Easter House

Loving

L isten to me

O ne way to be loving

V ery few people know

I s to be kind

N ever be nasty

G o and help people.

Tyler Grice (6)

Oakwood Primary School, Easter House

Happy

H appy is a new toy

A nd a cute puppy

P andas make me happy

P arties do too

Y ou make me happy.

Freya Iannelli (6)

Oakwood Primary School, Easter House

Star

S parkly stars shine down
T he teacher says I am a star
A nd so I try to shine
R eady to do my best.

Edie-Beau Bunton (6)

Oakwood Primary School, Easter House

Cool

C ody is cool
O nly tries his best
O ften is amazing
L ook at me!

Cody R (6)
Oakwood Primary School, Easter House

Gymnastics

G ymnastics keeps me fit and healthy

Y ou always have fun with your friends

M ats on the floor help me do a handstand

N ever give up if I do something wrong

A lways try my best

S winging on the bars makes me happy

T rampolines are really bouncy and enjoyable

I love gymnastics so much

C artwheels take time to learn

S o I have to be patient and just have fun

Sofia Vento (7)

Our Lady Of Lourdes Catholic Primary School, Finchley

Balloon

B alloons fly away in the blue sky
A rt is my favourite thing to do
L ight is really hot if you touch it
L adybird has black spots at the back
O range is one of my favourite colours
O ranges are so tasty
N umber one is the winner of the race.

Gabriele Marroccu (7)

Our Lady Of Lourdes Catholic Primary School,
Finchley

Donkey

D addy sometimes calls me Donkey for fun

O ranges are my favourite kind of fruit

N uts taste rotten to me

K arate is powerful to me

E xercise makes me strong

Y oghurt is what I have after food.

Patrick McErlean (7)

Our Lady Of Lourdes Catholic Primary School, Finchley

My Facts

N ever gives up

I nterested in lots of things

C urious about the world

O verwhelmed with joy

L oves drawing, reading and exploring

A lways busy doing something

S miles all the time.

Nicolas Junev (6)

Our Lady Of Lourdes Catholic Primary School, Finchley

Musicals

M elodramatic

U nbelievable

S kilful

I ncredible

C heerful

A bsorbing

L uminous

S o much fun.

Albert May (7)

Our Lady Of Lourdes Catholic Primary School, Finchley

Kara

K ids at a party
A pples Kara likes
R acing in the park
A lphablocks Kara likes too.

Nina Nyangeri (6)
Our Lady Of Lourdes Catholic Primary School,
Finchley

Lilly May

L emon is her favourite food

I nk is what she sometimes writes with

L yrics are what she sometimes sings

L imes are what she sometimes eats

Y ear of her birth is 2015

M eets people with a nice attitude

A pples are her second favourite food

Y esterday, she was a good girl.

Lilly Doyle (7)

Overstone Park School, Northampton

Necklace

N ever ugly
E xclusively lab created
C reated with love
K ind of extremely dazzling
L ovely
A masterpiece
C reation with passion
E very dazzle.

Dera Okafor (7)
Overstone Park School, Northampton

Spencer

S pider and snake lover

P layStation hater

E nergetic at my house

N ice when happy

C limbing up

E lephant lover

R oblox and Rocket League player.

Spencer Nathwani (7)

Overstone Park School, Northampton

Mitchell

M um is the best
I love her
T icking clocks
C at at home
H at is worn
E very day she wakes me
L indsey is happy
L itter is gross.

Mitchell Maskell (7)
Overstone Park School, Northampton

Jasmine

J am lover

A nice person

S assy girl

M iss Sneaky

I 'm never rude

N o broccoli

E lephant carer.

Jasmine Filbee (7)

Overstone Park School, Northampton

Hannah

H appy girl
A ctive moves
N ice person
N egative sometimes
A pples are my fave
H appy at all times.

Hannah Mabuto (7)
Overstone Park School, Northampton

Beaux

B ig bedroom

E very day I'm happy

A nd I love my koala quilt

U nder my quilt

X xxx, I love my mum.

Beaux Downing (7)

Overstone Park School, Northampton

Shamar

S uper
H i there
A lovely boy
M y toys are great
A nimals are good
R is in Shamar.

Shamar Hall (5)

Overstone Park School, Northampton

Garry

G ood boy

A lways clever

R eally happy

R uns fast

Y ou will like me.

Garry Denton (5)

Overstone Park School, Northampton

Basketball

B asketball is my favourite
A ll basketballs are good
S ometimes I am bad at basketball
K icking is not allowed
E verybody plays basketball
T all people
B asketball is fun
A ll tall people can play
L eaving is allowed
L ots of fun.

Abdur-Raheem Khan (6)
Prestwich Preparatory School, Prestwich

Football

F arhaan plays football with me

O n the pitch, I play a match

O n the pitch, I try to take the ball

T ackling is not hard

B all is what you play with

A güero has got a heart problem

L ionel Messi plays for Paris

L uke Shaw plays for Man United.

Hashim Zia (6)
Prestwich Preparatory School, Prestwich

I Am Taaliah

I am going to the park

A cat kicked me
M arch is spring

T aaliah is my name
A dog scratched me
A mouse wanted my food
L ucy is my best friend
I am good at dancing
A cat pinched me
H ashim bumped into me!

Taaliah Hamid (5)
Prestwich Preparatory School, Prestwich

Swimming

S wimming is fun

W ater is cool and fun

I like swimming because it is fun

M y favourite type of swimming is black float

M y cat likes water

I moved up a class

N ever want to stop swimming

G oggles stop you from getting water in your eyes.

Isla Gorman (6)

Prestwich Preparatory School, Prestwich

March

M oney buys big presents
A fter we cut the cake
R eal people came to the party
C ousins came to my party
H aving lots of fun.

Nkosi Kubekwani (6)
Prestwich Preparatory School, Prestwich

Maths

M aths is my favourite lesson
A dd up and take away
T imes tables are fun
H appy days at school
S chool is great.

Zayan Hussain (7)

Prestwich Preparatory School, Prestwich

Gaming

G ames

A game is fun

M y PS5 almost exploded

I love games

N o people do gaming

G ames are fun.

Samuel Dirawu (7)
Prestwich Preparatory School, Prestwich

Read

R eading is fun
E nglish is good
A story every day
D ancing with fairies.

Zaya Owoyomi (5)

Prestwich Preparatory School, Prestwich

Amber Milewska

A nimals are great

M y bestie is Nela

B ears scare me

E ven numbers are my favourite numbers

R aspberries are my favourite fruit

M y favourite animal is a meerkat

I am going to be a singer when I'm older

L ikes family so much

E ven I hate broccoli

W ent to Poland when I was five

S kyler is my favourite Rainbow High person

K arina is my best friend

A nimals are great.

Amber Milewska (7)

St Blasius CE Primary Academy, Shanklin

Nela Biesaga

N ew Years are happy for me
E ven I have a BFF, Amber
L ovely animals are cute for me
A nimals, I love chinchillas

B est fruit is grapes
I 'm the biggest chatterbox
E ven I have four people in my family
S o I love reading and playing
A year ago, we went to Poland
"G oo! Goo!" I said when I was a baby
A year ago, I loved my birthday.

Nela Biesaga (6)
St Blasius CE Primary Academy, Shanklin

Isla Lind

I 'm Isla and I love animals
S ome people like me because I'm clever
L ola is my best friend
A nimals are amazing

L ovely butterflies in the sky
I n my school, I've got lots of friends
N ot everyone knows me
D o you like cats?

Isla Lind (7)
St Blasius CE Primary Academy, Shanklin

Santiago

S antiago is my name

A nimals are my favourite

N ela is two chairs from me

T homas is my BF (best friend)

I love Jackson

A school is my favourite place

G eniuses are amazing

O ffspring are amazing.

Santiago Montenegro (6)
St Blasius CE Primary Academy, Shanklin

Beatrice

B eatrice is my name

E nglish is my favourite subject

A smiley person

T homas is my last name

R oller skates are good fun

I ris is my sister

C ats are fluffy, I like them

E verybody calls me Bea.

Beatrice Thomas (6)
St Blasius CE Primary Academy, Shanklin

Animals

A nimals are the best ever
N eed water, food and shelter
I like books about animals
M y favourite is a monkey
A ll animals are amazing
L ots of animals are smart
S o many animals in the wild.

Lincoln Newton (7)
St Blasius CE Primary Academy, Shanklin

Football

F ootball is fun on the pitch

O n a pitch

O f grass

T eams pass to each other

B alls are bouncy

A nd are always getting kicked

L ucky players in the

L eague score.

Jed Smith (6)
St Blasius CE Primary Academy, Shanklin

Malachi

M alachi is my name
A monkey is cool
L eopards are fast
A monkey is fast
C arrots help you see in the dark
H ats help you in the sun
I love my family.

Malachi Carman (7)
St Blasius CE Primary Academy, Shanklin

Rosie

R oses are my favourite flower
O ranges are my favourite fruit
S weets are my favourite food
I have a BFF called Isla
E lephants are my third favourite animal.

Rosie Kenny (6)
St Blasius CE Primary Academy, Shanklin

William

W illiam is my name
I like tigers
L ike running too
L ikes eating
I love playing with my dog
A nd I like sleeping
M y cat is friendly.

William Nicol (6)
St Blasius CE Primary Academy, Shanklin

Rhys

R unning is my third favourite thing to do
H awkeye is my fourth favourite superhero
Y o-yos are fun to play with
S uperman is my least favourite superhero.

Rhys Antoine-Neilson (6)
St Blasius CE Primary Academy, Shanklin

Elijah

E very day, I'm happy

L oves Monopoly

I like apples

J ackson is my friend

A nd so is Lyle

H aving friends is fun.

Elijah Simpson-Little (7)

St Blasius CE Primary Academy, Shanklin

Lacie

L oves wolves
A nd I like bananas
C ayman is my big brother
I can do the monkey bars
E very week I go to my stepmum's.

Lacie-Mae Firth (7)
St Blasius CE Primary Academy, Shanklin

Thomas

T he best about Thomas

H i, I am Thomas

O ne day I played

M y favourite game

A nd it is Mario

S uperstar.

Thomas Davey (6)
St Blasius CE Primary Academy, Shanklin

Olivia

O livia is my name
L ola is my best friend
I like my family
V ery much
I like dogs
A family is good.

Olivia Borkiewicz (7)
St Blasius CE Primary Academy, Shanklin

Fred

F red is my name
R ubies are bright red
E ating is my favourite hobby
D oesn't like pickles.

Fred Fry (6)
St Blasius CE Primary Academy, Shanklin

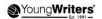

Lola

L ola loves dogs
O livia is my friend
L ola likes cute animals
A nd my family.

Lola Chambers (6)
St Blasius CE Primary Academy, Shanklin

Hugo

H ugo is my name
U nderground train
G oing to London
O n and off the lights.

Hugo Crates (7)
St Blasius CE Primary Academy, Shanklin

Ely

E ly is my name
L ie I never do
Y ou might meet me.

Ely Orchard (7)
St Blasius CE Primary Academy, Shanklin

Emily Keeler

E very fruit is my favourite
M y mummy makes me happy
I nteresting ideas in my head
L ove is happy to me
Y ummy food fills me up

K icking footballs make me happy
E very hug from Brody makes me feel
better when I'm sad
E lephants look fun to me
L ucie is so kind to me
E mily in Year 4 makes me laugh
R abbits are my favourite animal and dogs.

Emily Keeler (7)

Thomas Whitehead CE Academy, Houghton Regis

I Love Timeea

I love playing with Timeea

L ovely things I can do with Timeea
O utside is where we like to play
V iolets are my favourite flower
E verything is lovely with Timeea

T imeea is my bestie
I love Timeea
M e and Timeea love each other
E very day, we play together
E very day we have fun together
A pples are our favourite.

Eva Deme Dluhosova (7)
Thomas Whitehead CE Academy, Houghton Regis

Olivia-Mae

O n a good level of reading
L ove swimming, gymnastics and reading
I love Dalmatians
V ery nice and loving
I love Taylor Swift
A m in a good mood all the time
-
M aths is my favourite subject
A m always laughing with my mum
E ats porridge for breakfast.

Olivia-Mae Bogart (6)
Thomas Whitehead CE Academy, Houghton Regis

Football

F ootball is my thing

O ut on the pitch, I'm scoring loads

O ut on the wing, I'm running so fast

T elling friends, "You're really good!"

B elting shots. Goal!

A ll the time scoring lots

L ook, it's a goal!

L et's all celebrate.

Cameron Vickers (6)

Thomas Whitehead CE Academy, Houghton Regis

This Is Me

T alking to my friends at school
H aving to go to school a lot
I saac is my friend
S eeing teachers at school

I will try to score a goal in football
S eeing friends in my class

M eet my teachers at school
E at my breakfast every morning.

Samuel Dagnall (6)

Thomas Whitehead CE Academy, Houghton Regis

Kayleigh

K ind
A mazing teachers, friends and family
Y oung and adventurous
L oving and loyal
E nthusiastic in all they do
I love them all
G od's grace upon us all
H appy all the way.

Kayleigh Shumbambiri (6)
Thomas Whitehead CE Academy, Houghton Regis

Finley

F ins of a fish on the beach
I like eating McDonald's
N eed hugs every day
L ike spending time with family
v E ry good at football
lovel Y Mum and Dad.

Finley Long (6)

Thomas Whitehead CE Academy, Houghton Regis

Loving

L icking my ice cream
O pening my presents
V isiting my cousins
I love cuddling my cat
N ow I know what to do
G iving love to my family.

Kaiya Levey (6)
Thomas Whitehead CE Academy, Houghton Regis

Earth

E ating ice cream

A lways cuddling Tristan

R eally good at looking after my pets

T rying to improve doing the splits

H appy when I see a rainbow.

Mia Taylor (6)

Thomas Whitehead CE Academy, Houghton Regis

Earth

E ating ice cream
A lways on my tablet
R eally good at gymnastics
T rying to improve my gymnastics
H appy when I'm playing with my baby.

Lily (6)
Thomas Whitehead CE Academy, Houghton Regis

Earth

E ating ice cream

A lways watching my iPad

R eally good at writing

T rying to improve my basketball

H appy when I'm at home with my cat.

Scarlett Casey (6)
Thomas Whitehead CE Academy, Houghton Regis

Earth

E ating fruit
A lways playing with Mummy
R eally good at cuddling Mummy
T rying to improve my writing
H appy when it's sunny.

Millie Hedges (5)

Thomas Whitehead CE Academy, Houghton Regis

Earth

E ating ice cream

A lways doing karate

R eally good at remembering

T rying to improve backflips

H appy when making new friends.

Bailey Spencer Kennedy (6)

Thomas Whitehead CE Academy, Houghton Regis

Earth

E ating chocolate
A lways playing on Roblox
R eally good at reading
T rying to improve my writing
H appy when hugging Mum.

Erik Elek (5)

Thomas Whitehead CE Academy, Houghton Regis

Earth

E ating ice cream

A lways doing art

R eally good at reading

T rying to improve my writing

H appy when I see my nanny.

Ariana Rose Noka (6)

Thomas Whitehead CE Academy, Houghton Regis

Earth

E ating rice
A lways playing with my sister
R eally good at boxing
T rying to improve writing
H appy when swimming.

Darian Ukoh (5)
Thomas Whitehead CE Academy, Houghton Regis

Earth

E ating lunch

A lways running

R eally good at Roblox

T rying to improve my football

H appy when my mum cuddles me.

Michael Magnan (5)

Thomas Whitehead CE Academy, Houghton Regis

Jayda

J am is fruit on toast
A nimals make me happy
Y oghurts are yummy
D ogs are lovely
A ttention in the classroom.

Jayda Hart (7)
Thomas Whitehead CE Academy, Houghton Regis

That's Me

K ind and happy
A pples are yummy
D ad is the best
I love my teddy
E ver so lovely, this is me.

Kadie Lowe (6)
Thomas Whitehead CE Academy, Houghton Regis

YoungWriters® Est. 1991

Minecraft

M ining diamonds is fun
I n a cave you find stone
N o creepers in a cave
E ating carrots in Minecraft
C reating an enchanted pickaxe
R unning from an enderman
A n enchanted golden apple
F inding a cave
T ips in Minecraft.

William Sowtus (7)
Ysgol Ffordd Dyffryn, Llandudno

Christmas

C elebrate together
H olly on the tree
R eindeer in the sky
I cing on the cakes
S anta on the roof
T insel on the tree
M aking toys
A t home opening presents
S leigh on the roof.

Martha Guiney (6)

Ysgol Ffordd Dyffryn, Llandudno

Minecraft

M ining ancient debris
I n the night
N o looking at endermen
E nchanted sword
C reepers everywhere
R aid is coming
A pickaxe is used to mine
F un with players
T ime for cookies.

Gabriel Rodrigues (6)
Ysgol Ffordd Dyffryn, Llandudno

Minecraft

M ining for blocks

I nside a cave

N o going in lava

E xplode with TNT

C rafting a house

R unning from creepers

A t night

F ire to keep warm

T aking gadgets.

Louie Kincaid (7)
Ysgol Ffordd Dyffryn, Llandudno

Minecraft

M ine diamonds
I n a cave
N o creepers
E ndermen can't teleport
C raft a crafting table
R un from a creeper
A t night
F inding a village
T ime to play.

Barry Palin (6)

Ysgol Ffordd Dyffryn, Llandudno

Minecraft

M inecraft
I n the night
N ether portal
E meralds are green
C rafting table
R unning to the house
A ll the diamonds
F ires in caves
T owns by the desert.

Olly Owen (7)

Ysgol Ffordd Dyffryn, Llandudno

Family

F amily love each other
A ll together on walks
M eeting my family is fun
I s always kind
L ove to be together
Y ounger sister is nice.

Matilda Maddock (7)
Ysgol Ffordd Dyffryn, Llandudno

Family

F amily is always together
A ll together
M y family is the best
I love my family
L ove to watch films
Y ounger brother is cute.

Alisha Jubb (7)
Ysgol Ffordd Dyffryn, Llandudno

Roblox

R oblox is great
O bbies on Roblox
B uying clothes
L ove playing Roblox
O n Roblox, I play
e **X** tra Roblox.

Katelyn Jones-Gallagher (7)
Ysgol Ffordd Dyffryn, Llandudno

Gamer

G aming on Roblox

A dventures on games

M um plays games with me

E nchanted armour

R oblox is the best game.

Molly Jones (6)

Ysgol Ffordd Dyffryn, Llandudno

My Family

F amily all together
A lways walking to town
M y favourite time
I ce cream cones
L ove
Y ou.

Freya Vale (7)
Ysgol Ffordd Dyffryn, Llandudno

Family

F amily
A my is kind
M akes me happy
I like sharing
L ove all of them
Y ou are the best.

Eva Quinn (6)
Ysgol Ffordd Dyffryn, Llandudno

Cats

C ats are cute
A gile cats are quick
T ails are long
S miles all day.

Jessica Knight (7)
Ysgol Ffordd Dyffryn, Llandudno

King

K evin's dog

I s quick

N ice colour

G ood friend.

Kevin Cardoso Campos (6)
Ysgol Ffordd Dyffryn, Llandudno

Cat

C ats like running
A re soft and furry
T ry to jump and catch.

Sydney Woods (7)

Ysgol Ffordd Dyffryn, Llandudno